W9-AFJ-432

The Revolutionary War

VOLUME 4

❋ The ❋ Revolutionary War

VOLUME 4

The Spirit of 1776

James R. Arnold & Roberta Wiener

GROLIER

An imprint of

■SCHOLASTIC

Scholastic Library Publishing

www.scholastic.com/librarypublishing

First published 2001 by Grolier
An imprint of Scholastic Library Publishing
Old Sherman Turnpike
Danbury, Connecticut 06816

For information address the publisher:
Scholastic Library Publishing, Old Sherman Turnpike,
Danbury, Connecticut 06816

Reprinted in 2006

Library of Congress Cataloging-in-Publication Data

The Revolutionary War.
    p. cm.
  Contents: v. 1. The road to rebellion—v. 2. The shot heard around
the world—v. 3. Taking up arms—v. 4. The spirit of 1776—v. 5.
1777: A year of decision—v. 6. The road to Valley Forge—v. 7. War of
attrition—v. 8. The American cause in peril—v. 9. The turn of the tide
—v. 10. An independent nation.
    Includes bibliographical references and indexes.
   ISBN 0-7172-5553-0 (set)—ISBN 0-7172-5554-9 (v. 1)—
ISBN 0-7172-5555-7 (v. 2)—ISBN 0-7172-5556-5 (v. 3)—
ISBN 0-7172-5557-3 (v. 4)—ISBN 0-7172-5558-1 (v. 5)—
ISBN 0-7172-5559-X (v. 6)—ISBN 0-7172-5560-3 (v. 7)—
ISBN 0-7172-5561-1 (v. 8)—ISBN 0-7172-5562-X (v. 9)—
ISBN 0-7172-5563-8 (v. 10)
   1. United States—History—Revolution, 1775–1783—Juvenile
literature. [1. united States—History—Revolution. 1775–1783.]
  I. Grolier Incorporated.

E208 .R.47   2002   8673
973.3—dc21   2001018998

Printed and bound in Singapore

CONTENTS

CHAPTER ONE

The Strategy of 1776

George Washington's American army drove the British from Boston in March 1776. The British army sailed to safety in Halifax, Nova Scotia, Canada. There, the top British army commander in North America, General William Howe, waited for reinforcements from England. Meanwhile, he and other British leaders planned how to defeat the American rebels.

Because the Royal Navy controlled the seas, the British could land almost anywhere on the American coast. Once they landed, soldiers could build and defend a base. But to crush the rebels, the army would have to march inland and find and fight the Americans. After they left the coast or a large river, soldiers would not have the navy to supply them. Instead, they would have to use wagons to carry their supplies.

The Wagon Problem

The British army needed heavy four-horse wagons to carry most of its supplies. The wagons were like the big trucks of modern times. When the British got out of Boston, they had left behind about 100 of these wagons. The British government sent 300 new wagons across the ocean to replace that loss. The army also made special wagon yards at some of its bases in North America. There skilled craftsmen built new wagons. But all of those efforts were not enough. For the whole war the British army suffered from a shortage of wagons. Quite often the lack of wagons prevented the army from moving away from its base.

When the British army did move away from its base, the wagons carried the food, ammunition, and tents that the soldiers needed to survive. If possible, a chain of wagons connected the army with its base. When the wagons were empty, soldiers organized them into a

The British army faced a shortage of large four-horse wagons.

A rebel civilian defends his home.

group called a wagon train. The trains went back to the base to get more supplies. The trip back and forth to the base was dangerous because at any time American guerrillas might attack.

Guerrillas were soldiers who fought behind enemy lines. They did not wear uniforms but instead dressed in civilian clothes. That made it hard for the British to tell who was an enemy. The guerrillas gathered to attack a wagon train and then ran away to safety. That kind of fighting was called "hit and run."

The shortage of wagons and the guerrillas' hit-and-run attacks usually forced the British to stay close to their bases on the coast or on a river. One British colonel said that the problems of moving inland "prevented us this whole war from going fifteen miles" from a river or base on the coast.

The Shipping Problem

Almost all of the supplies the British army needed had to come from England: oats for the horses; salted beef and pork, flour, oatmeal, dried peas, and butter for the men. The British had to transport their supplies across 3,000

miles of ocean because the American colonies did not have enough to fill everyone's needs. Even in modern times, when ships use mighty engines to move through the water, a long supply line across the water still causes problems. During the Revolutionary War sailing ships depended on the wind to move. That made it much more difficult to keep the supply line working.

The North Atlantic has some of the world's worst storms. Sailing ships often met terrible storms. Some ships sank in the storms; others were damaged. It took sailing ships two to four months to complete the voyage across the Atlantic. By the time the ships arrived in America, many of the supplies were ruined. Yet each soldier in North America needed more than 600 pounds of food from England each year.

There were also not enough ships to carry men, horses, and supplies. Each battalion, a force with about 500 men, needed three or four troop ships simply to move. The official rules, or **regulations**, said that each battalion also could have 40 women. Some of the women were soldiers' wives. Their jobs included cooking and laundry. They too had to sail across the Atlantic. A British officer described the room in which his family lived during the voyage:

"Imagine to yourself a cube of 7 feet, that is 7 feet long, 7 broad, and 7 high, in this space only think of

> **regulations:** the printed official rules for all aspects of soldier behavior, army life, and conduct of military actions

Below: Transport ships carried supplies for the British army, including horses (shown on the lowest deck), across the Atlantic Ocean from England.

9

Messages

Germain sent 63 messages to one of his generals between May 1778 and February 1781.

Delivery Time	Number of Letters
under two months	6
2 months	12
2-3 months	28
3-4 months	11
4-5 months	4
5-7 months	2

stowing three women and three children, and to be at sea for 7 weeks: I believe you will hardly think it possible. But to explain it, on the right hand lay Mrs. Mac, in a bed 2½ feet wide, on the left Mrs. G, her bed about the same width, under her bed on the floor, her maid (a little, dirty, Scotch girl) over Mrs. G., her child in a cot about 2 foot long and 18 inches wide, which being suspended from the ceiling swung about with the motion of the ship; at Mrs. Mac's feet (in the same bed) lay Charlotte; in the space between the feet of the ladies beds . . . I had a little place (like a box without a cover) made up in which Fanny lay . . . I assure you that I was often afraid that some of them would be suffocated for want of fresh air. Only think of being cooped up in such a place when Mrs. G. was continually sick, even in the night, and throwing up every thing she attempted to take."

British military officers in America and government authorities in London needed to work together. The difficulty of sailing across the Atlantic Ocean also made it hard to communicate. A ship sailing from America usually had the wind blowing in the right direction. If all went well, it might take a month for news from America to reach London. A ship sailing west across the Atlantic had to battle the winds. It almost always took at least two months and often took three or four.

The Manpower Problem

The shipping problem was not the hardest problem

A dismounted British dragoon. The British army in America was always short of horses. One shipment left England with 950 horses. Four hundred horses died during the voyage across the Atlantic.

raise (an army): to build up a military force by getting new soldiers to enlist or by gathering soldiers from other units

facing the British government. Before it could even begin to win the war, the government had to find a way to **raise** thousands of new soldiers. General William Howe commanded the British army in North America. He told the British government that he needed 50,000 men. In 1775 there were about 29,000 soldiers in the entire British army. Ireland provided another 10,000. The soldiers were spread around British colonies in Africa, Europe, Canada, the West Indies, and America. There were many places to guard and too few soldiers to do the guarding.

It was hard to find volunteers in England who wanted to fight in America. Many Englishmen thought the Americans were like cousins. After all, most Americans

Throughout the war the British army faced problems finding food, horses, and wagons. This fact made British generals cautious. They knew that it took a long time to replace soldiers who were killed and supplies that were used up.

had come from England in the first place and still spoke the same language. British men did not like the idea of fighting against people who belonged to their own family.

So, the government offered money, called bounties, for men to join the army. There were also special gatherings, or patriotic appeals, where bands played, barrels of beer were served, and politicians made speeches to encourage men to volunteer.

One example took place in Dublin, Ireland. Major Boyle Roche told men that during the last war the British army had won every battle. He asked, "Will you, my dear Countrymen, permit those [victories] to fade or those actions to be forgotten?" He reminded them that there had never been a "more critical [time]" and said that the King was calling on them to serve at this crucial time. He concluded that "We have it in our power . . . to [defeat] those daring Rebels" and bring them "to a due Obedience to their [King] and [surrender] to the laws of their country." The words of Major Roche and men like him did not convince very many men to volunteer.

Since not enough men volunteered, the army looked in other places to find men. Men in prisons or in the poorhouses (a special type of prison for people who could not pay their bills) were given a choice: stay in prison or join the army. Many chose to join the army, but even so there were not enough men to supply all the 50,000 soldiers that Howe said he needed.

King George III and the government decided to hire soldiers. Soldiers who fight for money are called **mercenaries**. At first England tried to hire 20,000 Russian mercenaries. The ruler of Russia refused the offer. So England hired German mercenaries. In 1775 Germany was made up of many small countries instead of one larger country. They included places called Brunswick, Hesse-Cassel, Hesse-Hanau, Anspach-Bayreuth, Waldeck, and Anhalt-Zerbst. During the war the British hired almost 30,000 soldiers from those German countries. Because Hesse-Cassel supplied the most men, all of the German soldiers were called Hessians.

British Strategy

The British plan, or strategy, depended on going places where the Royal Navy could help the army. The strategy

mercenaries: soldiers who get paid to fight for a foreign country

had four parts. First, separate the New England colonies from the other colonies. To do so, the British wanted to seize the line of the Hudson River northward through Lake Champlain to the Canadian border. Second, isolate the central colonies, which grew the most food, from the rest of the colonies. To do that, the British wanted to hold Chesapeake Bay and the lower Susquehanna River. Third, control the southern colonies. To do that, the British wanted to capture and hold two ports in South Carolina, Charleston and Georgetown, and capture the line of the Santee River. Fourth, maintain a naval blockade of the American

German princes received money for each soldier they sent to America to help the British, so they sent their army to force men to join the Hessians.

Inset: German mercenaries belonging to the von Dittfurth regiment

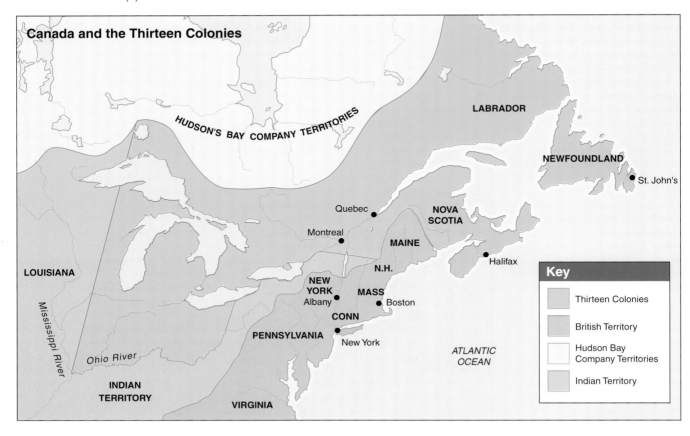

Canada and the Thirteen Colonies

HUDSON'S BAY COMPANY TERRITORIES

LABRADOR

NEWFOUNDLAND

St. John's

Quebec

NOVA SCOTIA

Montreal

MAINE

Halifax

N.H.

LOUISIANA

NEW YORK

MASS

Albany

Boston

CONN

PENNSYLVANIA

New York

ATLANTIC OCEAN

Mississippi River

Ohio River

INDIAN TERRITORY

VIRGINIA

Key

Thirteen Colonies

British Territory

Hudson Bay Company Territories

Indian Territory

coast to keep the rebels from importing weapons and supplies. The British strategy was fine. To make the strategy work, though, the British needed a large army and navy and leaders who could use the forces well.

The problems of finding enough ships, collecting enough supplies, and enlisting enough soldiers took time for Lord George Germain—the British Secretary of State for the American Colonies—and his government to solve. Germain hoped that all the reinforcements would be sent by the end of March. Instead, the first reinforcements for Canada did not sail until April 7 and 8. Howe's reinforcements did not begin to leave until April 29. Early in May another 9,200 British and Hessians sailed. Finally, in late June the last group of 7,000 Hessians left England.

Using mercenaries helped meet the manpower problem. Even with them, however, General Howe was short of the total that he wanted. By the middle of the summer of 1776 his army had about 30,000 British and Hessian soldiers.

CHAPTER TWO

The Campaign in Canada Ends

Back on the night of December 31, 1775, American forces had attacked Quebec, Canada. The battle ended with a bad American defeat. General Richard Montgomery was killed and Benedict Arnold wounded. The defeat discouraged the Americans. The terms of enlistment, or the time that the soldiers had to serve in the army, ended. Most men went home. Arnold was left with only about 100 men. He sent a messenger to Congress to ask for reinforcements and for a general to replace the fallen Montgomery.

Congress and George Washington did send more men to Canada. But sickness, desertion, and the end of more terms of enlistment kept the American force small. By the beginning of May 1776 about 500 healthy rebels were outside of Quebec, while 1,600 armed defenders supported by 148 cannons defended the city's walls. Then the ice covering the St. Lawrence River began to break up. On May 2, 1776, British reinforcements sailed up river. The Americans had no choice but to retreat.

The British commander, General Guy Carleton, attacked. The Americans fled, leaving behind 200 sick men, hundreds of muskets, and all of their artillery. More British reinforcements arrived to increase British strength to 13,000 men, including 4,300 Hessians. General John Burgoyne also arrived to serve under Carleton.

The British chased the Americans upriver toward Montreal. The American army fell apart. Hundreds of

The American soldiers suffered through a Canadian winter during which they had few supplies and little money to purchase what they needed.

men sickened with smallpox. The American commander died from the disease. A series of small battles took place, and the Americans lost all of them.

Because he had captured Boston back in March, Washington was able to send 2,000 good soldiers, including General John Sullivan, to help the American forces in Canada. Sullivan took command on June 1. Sullivan wanted to try to hold as much of Canada as possible. That was foolish because the British had a much bigger army. Benedict Arnold wrote to Sullivan, "Let us quit [Canada] and secure our own country before it is too late." Sullivan accepted his good advice. He ordered another retreat back to Lake Champlain. Arnold took command of the American rear guard, the soldiers whose job was to defend the backs of the retreating soldiers.

Sullivan's army limped back to Fort Ticonderoga. The army had suffered 5,000 casualties in Canada, including 3,000 men left behind because they were sick. John Adams visited the army and found it in very bad shape. Thousands were sick. Smallpox and malaria had weakened the army. Adams reported to Congress that the army was a horrible sight, "defeated, discontented, diseased, naked, undisciplined, eaten up with [insects]; no clothes, beds, blankets, no medicines."

The American invasion of Canada was over. Now it appeared that the British might invade American territory. Congress sent another general, Horatio Gates,

16

The battered rebels retreated from Canada back to Fort Ticonderoga. Both the patriot and the British armies followed the rivers through the wilderness because boats could carry their supplies.

to meet the British threat. The arrival of Gates angered General Sullivan. Sullivan believed that he, and no one else, should command in the area. So, Sullivan left the army, saying that he would resign.

The surviving Americans slowly recovered at Fort Ticonderoga. Militia and three regiments of Continentals (the regular American soldiers) reinforced them. Still, if the British had attacked quickly, there was little that the Americans could have done to stop them.

Instead, the British commander Carleton stopped at St. Johns, Canada. He had learned that the Americans had built a small fleet on Lake Champlain. Carleton needed to control the lake so that boats could carry his supplies down Lake Champlain. So, Carleton ordered his men to build a British fleet.

The Battle of Valcour Island

The effort to build the American fleet had come from Benedict Arnold. Arnold had been promoted to general

Some of the American boats and ships in Arnold's fleet.

Because of Benedict Arnold the rebels were able to build a small fleet to defend Lake Champlain.

for his conduct in Canada. Both he and General Gates understood that Lake Champlain was the key to the campaign in the north. Gates told Arnold to supervise the building of as many ships as possible.

Arnold again showed energy and skill. He offered special pay to attract skilled craftsmen who knew how to build ships. The craftsmen gathered at Skenesboro, New York, and worked through July and August. They built six flat-bottomed boats called gundalows. Each gundalow had a single mast and carried three guns and a 45-man crew. The craftsmen also built six larger ships called galleys. Each galley carried 8 to 10 guns with a crew of about 80 men. By the end of August Arnold led the fleet north toward the British.

Meanwhile, British craftsmen had also been busy. The Royal Navy had an 18-gun ship, the *Inflexible*, on the St. Lawrence River. Carleton ordered that it be taken apart and carried overland to Lake Champlain. There, British workers rebuilt the *Inflexible*. In addition, they built two small ships called schooners. One carried 12 guns, the other 14. They also built a 7-gun gondola, 20 small gunboats, and a giant raft called the *Thunderer*. The *Thunderer* carried heavy cannons and a 300-man crew. By the time the British finished work, they had a much more powerful fleet than the Americans.

The two fleets met on October 11, 1776, in a narrow channel between the mainland and Valcour Island. A hard fight took place. But the British *Inflexible* was too strong. It overpowered the smaller American ships. Night came. Arnold led his surviving

ships through the fog and past the British ships. In the morning the British chased the Americans. Arnold fought a gallant rearguard battle to try to let his fleet escape. The British forced Arnold to abandon most of his ships. The Americans set them afire to keep the British from capturing them.

The British were able to build bigger, more powerful ships to fight on Lake Champlain.

Arnold lost 11 of his 16 ships during and after the Battle of Valcour Island. The British gained control of Lake Champlain. Even though he had won the battle,

The Battle of Valcour Island, October 11, 1776.

Above: A rebel gun crew operates a cannon aboard one of Arnold's ships.

Carleton decided not to keep moving south. Winter would come soon, and he did not want to risk having to fight a campaign in the snow and cold. Instead, Carleton waited until the next year to attack Fort Ticonderoga.

That was a critical decision. If the British had captured Fort Ticonderoga in 1776, the fort would have served as the base for the campaign of 1777. If the British had started from the fort, the campaign of 1777 probably would have been successful. Instead, because of Arnold's effort to delay Carleton at the Battle of Valcour Island the British campaign of 1777 would have to begin with an attack against Fort Ticonderoga.

CHAPTER THREE

The Campaign for New York

Two brothers led the English military during the 1776 and 1777 campaigns. General William Howe commanded the army. Admiral Richard Howe commanded the Royal Navy in America. Admiral Howe had won a good reputation in the navy as an aggressive leader. Unlike most naval officers, Howe also cared about the common sailor. Like his brother, Admiral Howe was interested in helping his forces become more modern.

Opposite: Later in the war Benedict Arnold would turn traitor. He would always be remembered and hated for this treason. But in 1776 Arnold's actions on Lake Champlain may have saved the rebel cause.

Below: British soldiers land at Gravesend Bay, Long Island, on August 22, 1776.

Admiral Howe came to North America in July 1776. He had orders to strangle the rebels by blockading the American coast. He also had orders that named him as a peace commissioner to negotiate with the rebels. His brother was to assist him. This was a strange double mission. The Howe brothers were supposed to fight hard but at the same time be ready to talk about peace.

British strategy called for the capture of New York City, followed by an advance up the Hudson River. The transports carrying reinforcements across the Atlantic to

A soldier in Alexander Hamilton's New York artillery.

Halifax, Nova Scotia, were delayed by bad weather. When they finally arrived, General Howe realized that he would not have enough time to carry out the strategy. He decided that all he could do in 1776 was try to capture New York.

The first British convoy, or group of ships, arrived at New York City on June 29. Four days later British soldiers captured Staten Island without a fight. Then, General Howe decided to wait for all of his men to arrive before continuing. For weeks the number of British ships in New York Harbor grew. By the middle of July there were 10 ships of the line (the battleships of the time), 20 frigates (the cruisers of the time), and nearly 300 transports and supply ships. They carried almost 32,000 professional soldiers. However, only 24,600 were fit for duty. The rest were sick.

General George Washington was already in New York with most of the army that had driven Howe from Boston. In addition, Congress had worked hard to reinforce Washington's army. Congress had raised more Continental regiments from nearby states and ordered the militia to gather.

Their efforts gave Washington a paper strength of 28,500 men. (Paper strength means the number of soldiers whose names appear on a piece of paper called a muster.) However, many of those men were sick or absent. There were only about 19,000 men present and fit for duty. Most of them were new recruits or militia who were neither disciplined nor experienced in battle.

Washington faced a difficult problem. The city of New York stood on Manhattan Island. The Hudson, Harlem, and East Rivers surrounded New York. There was only one bridge, Kingsbridge (on the northern tip of Manhattan), joining New York with the mainland. Across the East River from Manhattan was Long Island. There rose Brooklyn Heights. If the British captured Brooklyn Heights, they could bombard the southern tip of Manhattan. That meant that the Americans had to defend Brooklyn Heights if they were to defend New York. However, British ships could sail up the East or the Hudson Rivers. They could cut off the American defenders on Long Island. The British control of the waters around New York gave the Howe brothers a huge advantage.

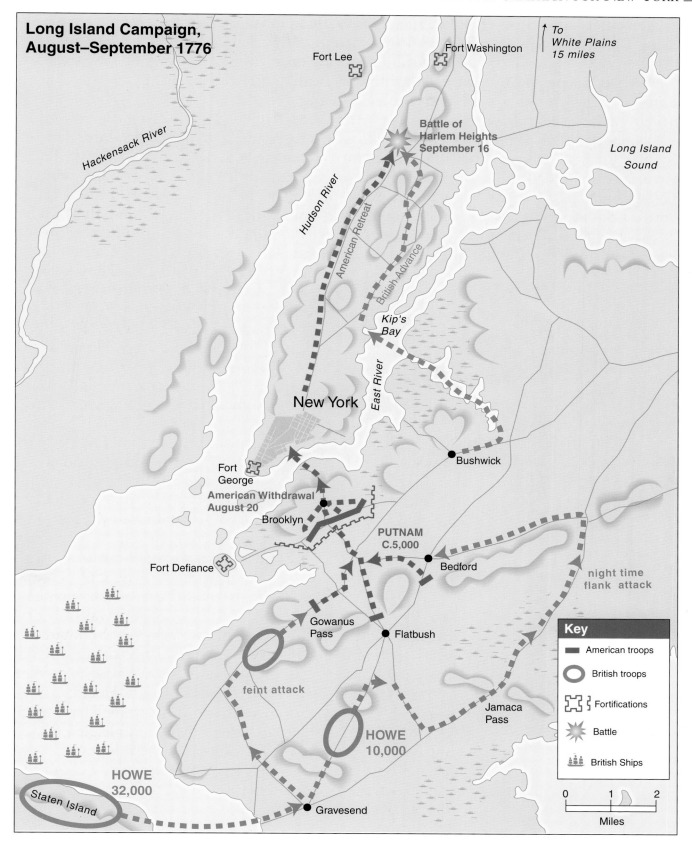

**Long Island Campaign,
August–September 1776**

Hackensack River

Fort Lee

Fort Washington

To
White Plains
15 miles

Battle of
Harlem Heights
September 16

Long Island
Sound

Hudson River

American Retreat

British Advance

Kip's
Bay

East River

New York

Fort
George

American Withdrawal
August 20

Brooklyn

Bushwick

PUTNAM
C.5,000

Bedford

Fort Defiance

night time
flank attack

Gowanus
Pass

Flatbush

feint attack

Jamaca
Pass

**HOWE
10,000**

Key

American troops

British troops

Fortifications

Battle

British Ships

**HOWE
32,000**

Staten Island

Gravesend

0   1   2

Miles

The Americans tried to keep the British ships from using the rivers. They sank ships in the rivers to block the channels. They built forts and batteries to shoot at any ships that passed by. The rebels did not know it, but none of those things would keep the British ships from moving wherever they wanted.

Washington sent about one-third of his army to Long Island. At first, a very good general named Nathanael Greene commanded the men on Long Island. Greene fell sick with malaria. General Sullivan, the officer who had left Fort Ticonderoga in a sulk, took charge. Just before the British attacked, Washington sent General Israel Putnam, one of the heroes of Bunker Hill, to take command.

The inexperienced American officers made many mistakes during the effort to defend New York.

On August 22, 1776, British infantry began landing on Long Island. Putnam placed the rebels on a long, narrow ridge that ran down the center of that part of Long Island. There were four passes, or places where roads passed over the ridge. Howe ordered a pretend attack, or feint, against Flatbush and Bedford Passes.

The feint worked. Putnam ordered most of his men to defend the passes. On the night of August 26 Howe led a 10,000-man force around Putnam's flank. The British marched through Jamaica Pass without meeting any Americans. In the morning the British made a new feint against Gowanus Pass. Putnam was completely fooled by their clever moves. When he finally realized that Howe had marched around his flank, he ordered a quick retreat. It was too late for the Americans defending Gowanus Pass. The British trapped them and forced them to surrender.

Washington was in New York City during these moves. He saw that things were going very badly. He crossed the river to join the discouraged army on Brooklyn Heights. Because the Royal Navy could sail up the East River and trap his men on Long Island, Washington should have ordered a retreat right away. But

Patriot forces withdraw after Howe marches around the rebel flank.

Above: Rebel artillery is loaded onto boats during the night-time evacuation of Long Island.

Washington was not yet an experienced army commander. He stubbornly ordered more men to join the forces on Brooklyn Heights. The American soldiers entered the trenches that had already been dug and waited for a British attack.

Howe looked at the situation. It reminded him of Bunker Hill. He did not want to risk an attack. Had he attacked, he probably would have captured most of the American army and maybe even Washington himself. Instead, Howe ordered his men to dig trenches and bring up heavy guns to begin a siege. Howe explained why he did not attack: "the most essential duty I had" was not to waste "His Majesty's troops....The loss of 1,000, or perhaps 1,500 British troops" in taking Brooklyn Heights "would have been but ill repaid" by the result. In other words, in Howe's mind the value of Brooklyn Heights was not worth the likely cost.

In the event, heavy rains slowed the British who were digging the trenches and moving the big guns. The delay gave Washington time to see that he had made a mistake. He ordered his army to retreat from Long Island on the night of August 29.

It was a desperate moment. If the Royal Navy discovered the American retreat, British warships could slaughter the rebels. A skilled and brave group of Massachusetts soldiers helped rescue the American army. Before the war the Massachusetts men had been fishermen living around the port of Marblehead. They manned the boats that carried the Americans. It helped that the night was foggy. The fog, and maybe the winds, kept the British ships from causing trouble. The entire American force escaped. They left behind six cannons.

Right: A boat evacuates George Washington from Long Island.

The Marbleheaders

Colonel John Glover of Marblehead, Massachusetts, was a wealthy merchant who owned trading ships. He was 42 years old when the American Revolution began. At this time Marblehead was a busy seaport. Glover recruited a regiment of fishermen and experienced sailors from the port. At sea sailors had to follow orders immediately and without question or risk endangering the entire ship. Because of this experience the men of this regiment were especially well disciplined and fearless.

The Marblehead regiment, called the Fourteenth Continental, served as foot soldiers in the Continental army. The regiment had about 500 men, and Glover's 20-year-old son commanded one of its companies. Former sea captains commanded some of the other companies. All but seven men of the original regiment were from Marblehead. Later, Glover had to recruit men from other Massachusetts towns to fill out the regiment. The men of the regiment wore uniforms that resembled the dress of sailors. Before Congress authorized the creation of a Continental navy, George Washington asked Glover to equip one of his own ships with guns. This ship went out to sea to raid British traders with a crew of soldiers from the Marblehead regiment.

On the night of August 29, 1776, Colonel Glover and his Marblehead men moved 9,000 soldiers across Long Island Sound. That feat saved them from certain capture. Again, on Christmas night 1776 the Marblehead regiment rowed George Washington's 2,400 men and their artillery across the ice-choked Delaware River to their history-making surprise attack on Trenton. That night the Marbleheaders had to fight ice, a strong current, waves caused by high winds, and a blizzard that made it almost impossible to see. Yet they did not lose a single man or a single cannon.

The fishing port of Marblehead, Massachusetts.

Once the Continental army arrived on the eastern bank of the Delaware, Glover and his men marched and fought along with the rest. Then, after the American victory the Marblehead regiment had to row nearly 1,000 prisoners back across the river in another dangerous night-time maneuver. A month later Glover received promotion to brigadier general. His brigade served at the Battle of Saratoga in 1777 and in Rhode Island in 1779.

The campaign for Long Island cost the Americans 1,012 men. The British lost only 392. General Howe had been more cautious than he should have been. Still, he had easily won the beginning of the campaign for New York.

The British hoped that the Americans loyal to the king, the loyalists, or Tories, would provide powerful help in the war against the rebels. As one British general put it, "I meant to assist the good Americans to [beat] the bad." The people of Long Island welcomed the British "with the greatest joy." Their welcome encouraged British leaders to believe that the loyalists would be a big help.

Peace Conference on Staten Island

The Howe brothers had used their forces to beat the rebels. The Americans had retreated to Manhattan Island. Admiral Lord Howe held the position of peace commissioner, the official who could negotiate with the rebels in order to try to end the fighting. The brothers decided that now was the time to try to make peace.

The British had captured General Sullivan during the Battle of Long Island on August 27, 1776. Lord Howe freed Sullivan so that the American could travel to Philadelphia and talk with Congress. On September 5 Congress decided to send a committee to explore peace with Howe.

Congress knew that King George had called the Americans traitors. The king believed that Congress was an illegal gathering. He refused to recognize that Congress held any authority. Congress knew that the king wanted the Americans to surrender and nothing else. They thought that maybe Lord Howe had the power to offer something better. So, Congress elected Benjamin Franklin, John Adams, and Edward Rutledge to go and meet with Lord Howe.

On September 11 the three Americans met with Lord Richard Howe on Staten Island. General William Howe was too busy making military plans to come to the meeting. Lord Howe made many promises about what he hoped would happen, about a happy peace between all of King George's subjects. The Americans quickly

Congress elected Benjamin Franklin, John Adams, and Edward Rutledge to meet with Lord Howe on Staten Island to discuss peace.

realized that Lord Howe did not really have the power to deliver what he promised. The real power was back in London. As Lord Howe reported back to London, "for very obvious reasons, we could not enter into any treaty with their Congress, and much less proceed in any conference" about American independence.

There was no reason for either side to keep talking. The Americans returned to Congress to report. Lord Howe returned to the business of defeating the Americans.

Harlem Heights

During the peace talks there was no fighting. The two-week delay should have helped the Americans rest and reorganize. Instead, the army began to fall apart. All the soldiers had begun to doubt that their generals were good enough to lead them in battle against the British. In fact, at that time many of the American generals were bad leaders. The militia were especially discouraged by the recent defeat. Many decided to go home. The Connecticut militia shrank from 8,000 to 2,000 men in just a few days. Washington was left with about 20,000 men, including 5,000 soldiers too sick to fight.

Washington faced the big decision about whether to defend Manhattan. Nathanael Greene, who had recovered from malaria and returned to duty, argued

British ships controlled the waters around New York City.

that New York City should be burned and abandoned. Burning the city would make it useless for the British. Several other officers agreed, including John Jay. Jay was a wealthy man, and most of his wealth was in land and buildings in New York. But Jay was a great patriot who put the cause of freedom ahead of his own wants.

However, Congress refused to let the city be burned. So, Washington decided to defend Manhattan. That was a mistake. The British could move freely along the rivers surrounding Manhattan. Just as on Long Island, the British could trap Washington's army.

Washington placed most of his men near Harlem Heights toward the north end of Manhattan Island. He left General Putnam with 5,000 men in the city at the south end. Greene commanded a group of militia guarding the East River in the center. In other words, Washington spread his army out over sixteen miles with his weakest force in the middle. That too was a mistake. Washington was still learning how to use his army.

During the night of September 15 British warships moved up the East River and anchored 200 yards off Kip's Bay. The sailors heard American guards on shore shouting to one another, "All is well." The sailors shouted back, "We'll [change] your tune before tomorrow night."

Hessian soldiers were part of the British army that entered New York City. This drawing shows them marching through the city and appeared in a German publication.

At about 11 A.M. the warships opened fire on the American militia defending Kip's Bay. The heavy fire scared the militia. At first a few militia ran away. Soon more and more followed. By the time the British infantry landed, all of the militia had fled. A British general bragged, "the rogues [the Americans] have not learnt manners yet, they cannot look gentlemen [the British] in the face." Washington and his officers tried to rally their troops, or stop them from running. The militia refused to stop until they were far away from the fighting.

Washington sent orders to Putnam to leave the city. Everyone knew that if the British hurried, they could move south across Manhattan and trap Putnam. Indeed, Putnam almost led his men into a trap. At one point the distance between Putnam and the British was no greater than the width of today's Central Park. But Putnam's aide, Aaron

According to patriot legend Mrs. Robert Murray helped save the American forces in Manhattan. The story was told that she invited British officers into her home and entertained them with wine and food. By delaying the officers, she gave the American forces time to escape from the city. The charming legend probably is more fairy tale than fact.

Burr, led the men to safety. Still, the Americans had to leave behind their cannons and many supplies.

The next day, September 16, the American army took a position on Harlem Heights. There the rebels had built fortifications and dug trenches. Washington ordered a scouting mission to find out what the British were doing. Colonel Thomas Knowlton, the officer who had skillfully defended the rebel left flank at Bunker Hill, commanded the scouts.

Knowlton's Connecticut Rangers met a group of elite British light infantry and a unit of the famous 42nd Highlanders, the "Black Watch." The rebel rangers fired about eight volleys before retreating. Washington heard the sounds of battle. He rode to see what was happening. As he arrived, Knowlton's men were still retreating. The British light infantry were chasing them. The light infantry used bugle calls to send messages. To Washington and his aides it sounded like a fox hunt, with the British the hunters and Knowlton's men the fox. Joseph Reed was there, and he wrote that he had never felt such an awful feeling before, "it seemed to crown our disgrace." Reed meant that their defeat came on top of the recent defeats at Long Island and Kip's Bay.

The battlefield of Harlem Heights from a photo taken more than 100 years after the battle. At the time of this photo New York City still had rural areas.

Perhaps the sound of the bugle made Washington mad. He ordered some nearby Continentals to attack the British. Washington formed, or placed, his soldiers to trap the British if they continued to charge ahead. Washington's plan worked. A small battle took place. When it was all over, the Americans had lost about 30 killed and 100 wounded and missing. Thomas Knowlton, an officer who had shown great talent, received a mortal wound (a wound that leads to death). British losses were about 14 killed and 154 wounded.

The importance of the Battle of Harlem Heights was not the number of men killed and wounded. More important was the fact that unlike the recent battles, the Americans had stood and fought. They had hurt the British as much as they had been hurt themselves. The morale, or spirit, of the entire American army rose after the battle. An American officer wrote to his wife, "The men have recovered their spirits and feel a confidence which before they had quite lost." The battle especially encouraged Washington. He wrote that the fight had "inspired" the rebels. "They find it only requires [determination] and good officers to make an enemy give way."

The Battle of Harlem Heights, September 16, 1776 .

CHAPTER FOUR

Disaster at Fort Washington

George Washington and his army had survived two traps while trying to defend New York. Washington did not learn enough from the experience. For the next month he kept his army in position on Harlem Heights. If the British moved to capture Kingsbridge, north of Washington's position, they could trap the entire American force.

But General Howe was not a man to move quickly. He also had some problems of his own. Howe had planned to house, or quarter, his soldiers in New York City during the winter. Shortly after midnight on September 21 a house fire broke out in the city. The wind caused the fire to spread rapidly. By the time

Above: Scottish Highlanders at the Battle of Harlem Heights.

British soldiers and New York civilians had put the fire out, it had destroyed 493 houses. Some American officers had wanted to burn the city before they abandoned it. The New York City fire was an accident. But Washington was pleased. He said that it "has done more for us than we were [ready] to do for ourselves."

Below: The great fire in New York destroyed many buildings.

A brilliant inventor, David Bushnell, designed a capsule that a single man could propel using his feet. It moved just beneath the water and could dive beneath the surface. It carried a time bomb that could be attached to the side of an enemy ship. The capsule was about 7.5 feet long and 6 feet in height and was known as the *Turtle*.

Howe had learned the lesson of Bunker Hill. He did not want to attack the rebels when they were defending earthworks (trenches and small forts built with dirt walls). So, he decided to move around, or outflank, the American position on Harlem Heights. On October 12 Howe sent 4,000 men by ship to Throg's Neck. That was a poor choice. There was only one narrow road across the marshes that led inland from the river. A small group of Pennsylvania riflemen defended the only bridge. Howe was not sure what to do. Meanwhile, the Americans sent reinforcements. After six days Howe gave up his plan to move inland from Throg's Neck.

Howe's next try came at Pell's Point on October 18. Again the British moved by ship to outflank the Americans. Four thousand redcoats marched inland from Pell's Point. They met a brigade of 750 Americans at Eastchester. Colonel John Glover, the officer who commanded the Marblehead, Massachusetts, regiment that had saved the army on Long Island, commanded the rebels. Even though Glover was outnumbered, he fought skillfully. His brigade fired and fell back, and then fired again. That type of battle was a rearguard battle (a fight with the goal of slowing the enemy so the army can retreat safely). Like the Battle of Harlem Heights, that skirmish showed that some Americans were becoming good soldiers.

The British landing at Pell's Point outflanked Washington's position on Manhattan. Washington saw that he had to retreat. Glover's rearguard fight gave him the time to march to safety. Washington marched his army north to White Plains, New York. Finally, the American army was free from the trap on Manhattan Island. However, Washington knew that Congress wanted him to hold Manhattan if he possibly could. So, he left about 2,800 men at a place called Fort Washington on the north end of Manhattan.

Howe continued with his cautious, slow way of making war. He did not move to fight Washington for another week. On October 28 Howe marched toward White Plains. For the first time in the campaign the two armies met one another away from a place where the British navy could help the British army. Howe's army numbered 14,000 men. He had left another 8,000 men to guard his base back on the coast at New Rochelle. Another British force guarded New York City.

The split in the British forces showed the problem the British faced. To win the war, the British needed to defeat the main American armies and to occupy the important American cities and towns. As soon as the British army moved inland to find and fight the Americans, it became weaker because it had to leave large forces to guard its rear. The farther inland the British marched, the weaker they became because they had to leave guards at all the important places.

At White Plains Washington's army numbered about 14,500 men. So the two armies were nearly equal. However, the quality of Howe's army was much higher. They were all professionals, while the American force had many militia and new recruits. Once again the

The *Turtle* made its first attack on September 7, 1776, against the H.M.S. *Eagle,* a 64-gun ship of the line that was anchored in New York harbor. The try failed when the screw used to attach the time bomb struck an iron plate on the *Eagle*'s hull.

Americans dug trenches and built earthworks to defend White Plains. Once again Howe moved around the American flank. A sharp fight took place, and yet again the American Continentals fought well and the militia ran. Howe captured an important hill on the American flank. That forced Washington to retreat northward, away from New York City. Rather than chase Washington, Howe marched west to Dobb's Ferry on the Hudson River. His army was now between Washington's army and the garrison at Fort Washington.

Washington was in a difficult situation. On November 6 he held a meeting, or council of war, to decide what to do. Washington thought that Howe was about to invade New Jersey. But Howe could also move into New York or even Connecticut. In order to defend all the rebel territory, Washington and his generals decided to divide the army into four parts.

General Charles Lee had returned from his mission in Charleston, South Carolina. Washington gave Lee

The British captured the 21-year-old rebel spy, Nathan Hale, during a mission in New York. Before his execution on Sepetember, 22, 1776, Hale said, "I only regret that I have but one life to lose for my country."

Prisoners of War

Both the British and the Americans took thousands of prisoners during the American Revolution.

The Americans captured about 1,000 men at Trenton in 1776, 5,000 at Saratoga in 1777, and 8,000 at Yorktown in 1781. The British took about 4,000 American prisoners in the New York campaign in 1776 and more than 5,000 at Charleston in 1780. Neither army had enough places to keep so many prisoners, nor did they have enough food for them. The numbers of prisoners decreased as some died, escaped, were exchanged, or agreed to join the enemy's army or navy. While in prison, prisoners constantly tried to escape. Many dug tunnels under the prison walls. When the guards found a tunnel, they would put the diggers in solitary confinement. This did not frighten the other prisoners. They soon started digging another escape tunnel.

The British crowded their American prisoners into buildings and prison ships around New York City. A prison ship offered the possibility of escape for anyone who could jump overboard and swim away. But very few people could swim in those days. Spoiled food and crowded conditions caused disease and death. An estimated 11,000 American prisoners of war died on the British prison ships anchored around New York during the Revolution. If this estimate is correct, that is more than were killed by British guns.

The Jersey prison ship has gone down in history as the most infamous of the British prisons. It held more than a thousand prisoners at a time. Each morning

Sick and weak patriot prisoners inside the Jersey.

the prisoners were ordered, "Rebels, turn out your dead," and those who had died during the night were removed from the ship and buried on shore.

The British also took American prisoners from Continental navy ships they captured at sea. Navy men captured at sea were taken to prisons in England. The prisoners did not get enough to eat. An American seaman who kept a prison diary wrote: "It is enough to break the heart of a stone to see so many strong, hearty men, almost starved to death. . . . Many are strongly tempted to pick up the grass in the yard, and eat it . . . . Some will pick up snails out of holes in the wall, and from among the grass and weeds in the yard, boil them and eat them."

command of the largest part, about 6,000 to 7,000 men. Lee's mission was to stop Howe from invading Connecticut. A 4,000-man force commanded by Major General William Heath moved about 30 miles north to an area called the Hudson Highlands. That was an area the rebels had to hold to keep the British from moving up the Hudson River and dividing the colonies into two. General Greene took charge of the 3,500 soldiers guarding Fort Washington and another fort named Fort Lee that was just across the river on the New Jersey side of the Hudson River. Washington himself moved to New Jersey to take command of a reserve force.

Dividing his army into four parts was bad strategy. None of the parts could help, or support, the other parts. The Hudson River divided the American forces. The purpose of Fort Washington and Fort Lee was to stop British ships from sailing north up the Hudson

British boats carry infantry and guns across the Hudson River to the New Jersey shore on November 20, 1776. A column of infantry climbs a steep foot path to the top of the New Jersey Palisades, from where they marched against Fort Lee.

River. But British warships had already shown that they could sail past the forts. So, there was no reason to have American soldiers stay in the forts. But Nathanael Greene believed that the forts could be defended, and Washington trusted Greene.

The scene was set for a disaster. It came on November 16 when Howe attacked Fort Washington. A tough battle took place before the British and Hessians captured the fort. One Scottish Highland officer gleefully told the American prisoners, "Ye Should Never Fight Against Yer King." During the fighting the Americans lost 59 killed and 96 wounded. The British and Hessians lost 84 killed and 374 wounded. However, the British captured 230 rebel officers and 2,607 men along with 36 pieces of artillery.

Most of the prisoners came from the states south of New England. The defeat made them bitter. They believed that Greene, a New Englander, would never have sacrificed them if they too had been New Englanders. All but 800 of those prisoners were to die in British prison camps.

Four days after the victory at Fort Washington the British crossed the Hudson River to attack Fort Lee. Washington had wisely ordered that fort abandoned. The garrison, or men defending the fort, escaped. But they left behind many valuable supplies.

So the campaign for New York ended with a big British victory. Since the Battle of Long Island Washington had lost hundreds of men killed, more than 4,400 taken prisoner, and much precious equipment and supplies.

The situation was very bad for Washington and his army. Whenever things went badly, many if not most of the militia left the army to go home. One of Washington's aides saw the militia jamming the roads and "returning to their homes in the most [cowardly] manner." All of the Massachusetts militia would complete their terms of service on November 17. The Continentals raised by Congress were due to go home at the end of November or December. Washington was left with only about 3,500 discouraged soldiers. Howe had close to 30,000. If Howe could finish off Washington, the war would be over.

CHAPTER FIVE

"The American Crisis"

In many ways the delegates to the Continental Congress behaved as if they did not understand the problems faced by George Washington and his army. Congressmen debated the question of having a professional army. They used the term "standing army" to mean professional army. Most of the delegates feared a standing army.

Most American leaders came from English families. Their families had left England at a time when the government used the military, the standing army, to take away people's civil and religious freedoms. The delegates had gone to school and learned history. History taught them that many great nations, such as the Roman Empire, had lost their freedoms to standing armies. The delegates did not want that to happen in America. For that reason delegate John Adams said to an American officer in June 1776, "We don't choose to trust you generals, with too much power, for too long a time."

General Washington learned that he needed to have power to fight the war. After the British defeated him twice, he wrote to Congress. He said that the army needed new rules. Without new rules he could not discipline the army. Unless he had disciplined soldiers, he could not fight the British and Hessian professional soldiers.

Toward the end of September 1776 Washington again wrote to Congress. He explained that the army needed to recruit soldiers for a longer term of enlistment. Training a soldier took time. By the time a soldier had learned what he needed to know, his term of enlistment

A rebel recruiting poster inviting "All brave, healthy, able bodied, and well disposed young men" to join Washington's army.

had nearly ended. For example, in September Washington commanded some good, trained Continentals. But he knew that most of them were about to leave the army and go home.

Washington explained to Congress that because of the short terms of enlistment, he had to depend on the citizen soldiers, the militia. But the militia had run on Long Island and again at Kip's Bay. If he had to rely on the militia, it was like "resting upon a broken [crutch]." Washington concluded his letter by saying that the fear of a standing army was like being afraid of something far away. Meanwhile, the lack of an American standing army was causing a huge danger that was very close. He wrote that there must be a complete "change in our military systems."

Congress had great faith in Washington. Delegates took his words seriously. They held meetings to think about what to do. Delegates debated all sorts of plans. They finally came up with a plan to raise a new army. But that plan had many problems. It would take a long time to work. It let politicians in all the colonies choose officers to lead the new army. Washington knew that the politicians were more likely to pick their friends and that their friends might not be good military leaders.

One of Washington's generals, Charles Lee, thought that he knew what to do. Lee blamed Congress for all of the army's troubles. He wrote to a congressman, "Had I the

Before the defeats around New York soldiers were more willing to join the Continental army. A Maryland Continental regiment departs Annapolis, Maryland, to serve with Washington.

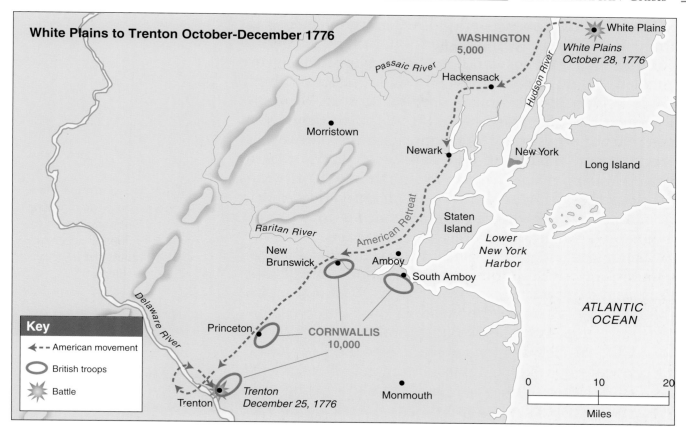

White Plains to Trenton October-December 1776

powers I could do you much good...but I am sure you will never give any man the necessary power." Lee thought that Congress should appoint one man and give that man all the power. In other words, Congress should name someone a dictator. Washington did not know it, but Lee believed that he, Charles Lee, should become dictator.

Chase through Jersey

After the loss of Fort Washington and Fort Lee Washington's army was split into many groups. The two largest groups were east of the Hudson River. Charles Lee commanded 7,000 at White Plains. His job was to keep the British from moving into New England. General Heath commanded 4,000 men at Peekskill, New York. Heath's job was to guard the Hudson River. A force of 1,000 men guarded the New Jersey coast against British raids. That left Washington with only about 3,500 men. On November 20, 1776, Washington's small army was at Hackensack, New Jersey.

On the British side General Howe had to decide what to do next. Winter would come soon, bringing snows to end the campaign season. Before that happened, Howe decided to do two things. He sent General Henry Clinton with a 6,000-man force to capture Newport, Rhode Island. Newport would give the British fleet a safe harbor to escape from winter storms. Howe also sent General Charles Cornwallis with 5,000 men to chase Washington through New Jersey. Cornwallis bragged that he would catch Washington just like a hunter on a horse with a pack of hunting dogs catches a fox.

Washington knew that he was in trouble. He needed Charles Lee to send reinforcements from White Plains. But Lee did not want to cooperate with Washington. Lee thought up excuses for not sending the reinforcements. Washington had no choice but to order his army to run for its life. So began a long retreat through New Jersey.

Cornwallis chased hard. His men marched 20 miles in a single day through heavy rain. They almost caught the rebels at Brunswick, New Jersey. The Americans escaped

The Hessian Jagers were the only British unit to carry rifles. They were excellent soldiers.

across the Raritan River with the British close behind them. The rebels tried to burn the bridge but some fast-moving Hessian Jagers (a German word for light infantry that means hunter) put out the fire before the bridge was destroyed.

The people of New Jersey watched Washington's small army retreat. To them it looked like a defeated army. At that time General Howe published an offer saying that if the Americans stopped fighting, they would not be punished. Many New Jersey men thought that it was a good idea to accept Howe's offer. When Washington called for the New Jersey militia to gather, almost all refused. Another 2,500 New Jersey men went to the British camps to enlist in the British army.

Washington led his discouraged men south and west to the Delaware River. He reached Trenton on December 3. Washington learned that Charles Lee had finally followed orders and was marching to join him. But Lee was still several days away. On December 7 Washington retreated across the Delaware into Pennsylvania. He gathered or destroyed all of the boats on the river so that the British could not cross the Delaware and attack him.

On December 12 delegates to the Continental Congress met in Philadelphia. They knew that Cornwallis and the British army were getting near. Since Philadelphia was no longer safe, the delegates decided to move to Baltimore, Maryland. Before fleeing, the delegates voted to give Washington "full power to order and direct all things" connected to the military. That was the power Washington needed, but to many it seemed that Congress had made the decision too late. Washington still had hope. He told an officer, "If we can [gather] our forces together...we may yet [make] an important [fight]."

The next day, December 13, a group of British cavalry called light dragoons captured General Charles Lee at

During the retreat through New Jersey soldiers such as this footsore man at the bottom of the picture became even more discouraged. In the middle of the picture Washington tries to persuade his men to stay with the army.

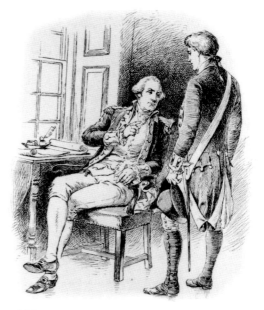

When the army reached the Delaware River, Washington ordered all the boats collected so that Cornwallis could not cross the river.

49

British dragoons surprise and capture General Charles Lee at Basking Ridge, New Jersey.

Basking Ridge, New Jersey. That same day General Howe announced that he was done campaigning. His forces had driven almost all of the rebels out of New Jersey. Howe ordered his men to move to towns where they could find shelter for the winter (that is called going into winter quarters). Howe himself returned to New York City.

While chasing the rebels, Cornwallis's forces had entered Trenton. The Delaware River flowed by Trenton. Howe thought that Cornwallis should move back from the Delaware River. Cornwallis argued that a retreat would discourage the New Jersey loyalists. Cornwallis wanted to keep all of the territory that he had captured. He added that Washington's forces were not dangerous. So, Howe let Cornwallis keep British and Hessian forces at two towns on the river, Bordentown and Trenton. Cornwallis's main base was at Brunswick with a smaller base at Princeton.

While the British and Hessians went into winter quarters, the rebel army continued to fall apart. Washington knew that most of his soldiers were at the end of their enlistments. At the end of December they would go home. Washington had tried hard to convince Congress to make a new army. His efforts did not seem to be working. On December 18, 1776, Washington wrote to his brother that unless something changed soon, "I think the game is pretty near up."

Thomas Paine was 39 years old. He had marched with Washington's army during its long retreat across New Jersey. Paine had shared the soldiers' suffering. The soldiers' devotion to the cause of freedom inspired Paine. Paine thought about what he was seeing and

Thomas Paine

Thomas Paine was born in England in 1737. He went to grammar school for six years, then, at the age of 13 he became an apprentice in his father's trade, making corsets (a type of women's underwear). After six years as an apprentice he ran off to sea on a British privateer. (A privateer was a kind of ship that chased and captured the trading ships of England's enemies and allowed the sailors to keep and sell the contents.)

When Paine's ship returned eight months later, he worked at corset-making and a variety of other jobs but could not make a good living. Meanwhile, he educated himself by going to lectures and reading books. He fell in love and married a poor woman, an orphan who worked as a maid, but his wife died in childbirth the next year. It would be twelve years before he married again in 1771.

Desperate for a way to make a living, Paine found work as a tax collector. He lost his job because he was falsely accused of dishonest practices. He ran a tobacco shop and campaigned to get his job back, which he finally did. Then in 1772 he lost the job for good when he wrote a pamphlet arguing that tax men deserved higher pay. This was Thomas Paine's first piece of writing in which he argued for a cause. He went to London to present his argument. However, as a reward for his efforts he went broke and separated from his wife. One good thing came out of his trip to London. He met Benjamin Franklin. Franklin convinced him to go to America.

In 1774, at the age of 37, Thomas Paine arrived in Philadelphia. He found a job writing for a new magazine, which became very popular, but Paine argued with the owner and quit. Inspired by the spirit of revolution in the land, in January 1776 he wrote his best-known pamphlet, "Common Sense," which argued for independence from England. Even though many people thought his ideas were too radical, hundreds of thousands of copies were sold. Paine refused to accept money for writing "Common Sense." He asked that any money made from selling copies be used to buy warm clothing for Continental soldiers. In July 1776 Thomas Paine joined the Continental army. He continued to write about the Revolution while he was a soldier.

Thomas Mifflin provided an important service when he worked hard to raise militia to join Washington.

wrote a short letter that he called "The American Crisis—Number One." Paine's letter appeared in the *Pennsylvania Journal* on December 19. The first paragraph read:

"These are the times that try men's souls. The summer soldier and the sunshine patriot will, in this crisis, shrink from the service of their country; but he that stands it now, deserves the love and thanks of man and woman. Tyranny . . . is not easily conquered; yet we have this consolation . . . that the harder the conflict, the more glorious the triumph."

Rebel soldiers read or listened to the reading of Paine's glorious words. The words filled the soldiers with pride and courage. They were determined to do their duty.

So far during the war Pennsylvania had not given very much to the rebel cause. General Thomas Mifflin traveled through Pennsylvania to stir up support for the war. Mifflin's efforts were later called "one of the most important missions of the war." Mifflin was able to convince many Pennsylvania people to help the army.

On December 20 General Sullivan led 2,000 tired soldiers into Washington's camp. They had come from White Plains, New York. They were all the men who were left from a force of 5,000 men that had crossed the Hudson River from New York with General Charles Lee. General Horatio Gates brought 500 men from upstate New York. Colonel John Cadwalader joined with 1,000 special militia called the Philadelphia Associators. Colonel Nicholas Haussegger brought the German Battalion, a unit of German-speaking Americans from Maryland and Pennsylvania. With those reinforcements Washington's army grew to around 6,000 men.

Washington knew that after December 31 he would be left with only 1,400 men. He decided to make an attack before that date. He chose the Hessian soldiers quartered in Trenton, New Jersey, as his target.

CHAPTER SIX

Nine Glorious Days:
The Battles of Trenton and Princeton

Washington planned his attack carefully. He knew that Christmas Day was special for the Hessians. For them it was a day of eating, drinking, and going to parties. Washington figured that by the night of December 25-26 the Hessians would not be paying close attention to their military duty. Washington planned to take advantage by attacking the Hessians early in the morning on December 26 while it was still dark.

Washington himself would lead 2,400 soldiers against Trenton. The soldiers would cross the Delaware River in boats and then make a march during the night to Trenton. Meanwhile, a group of militia would cross the river elsewhere to block a Hessian retreat. Finally, Colonel Cadwalader would lead 2,000 men across the river to attack Bordentown.

Washington's plan depended on the weather. If it was too cold, the river would freeze, and the boats would not be able to carry the rebels across the Delaware. If it stormed too hard on the night of December 25-26, his soldiers would be unable to march. Even while Washington made his final plans, the weather grew worse. Washington did not know it, but the bad weather stopped both Cadwalader and the rebel militia. That left Washington's force alone to make the attack.

The 2,400 men, along with 18 cannons commanded by Henry Knox, left the American camp at 2 P.M. on Christmas Day. The soldiers got on the boats in the dark. Glover's Marblehead regiment, the same soldiers who had rowed the army to safety from Long Island

A Hessian grenadier belonging to von Rall's regiment.

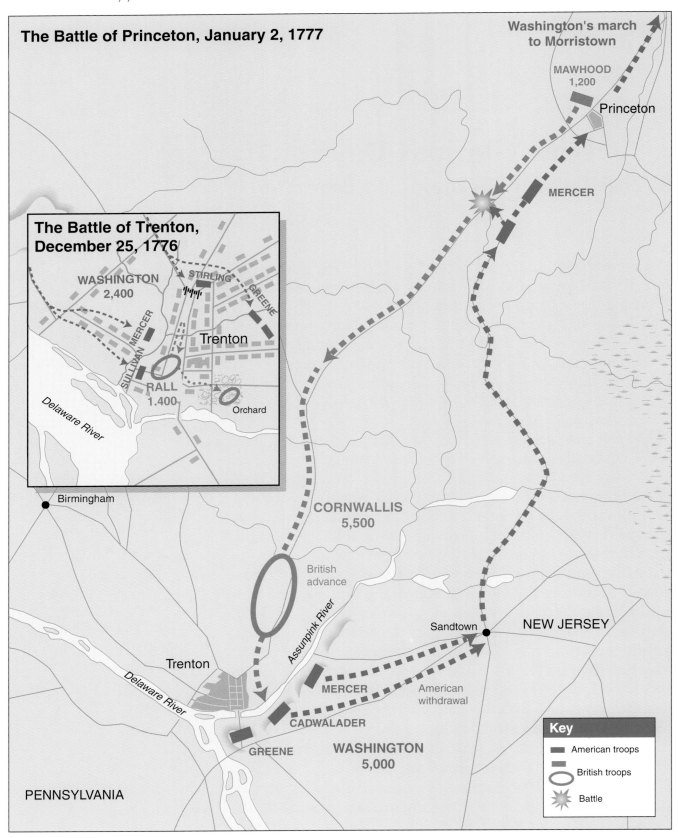

The Battle of Princeton, January 2, 1777

Washington's march to Morristown

MAWHOOD
1,200

Princeton

MERCER

**The Battle of Trenton,
December 25, 1776**

WASHINGTON
2,400

STIRLING

GREENE

MERCER

Trenton

SULLIVAN

RALL
1,400

Orchard

Delaware River

Birmingham

CORNWALLIS
5,500

British
advance

Assunpink River

Sandtown

NEW JERSEY

Trenton

MERCER

American
withdrawal

Delaware River

CADWALADER

GREENE

WASHINGTON
5,000

PENNSYLVANIA

Key
American troops
British troops
Battle

back in August, rowed the rebels across the Delaware. It was a dangerous trip. The river ran fast. There was floating ice. About 11 P.M. a storm began bringing rain, hail, and snow. The weather slowed the crossing of the river. The army was supposed to be across by midnight. In fact, it was not ready to march on Trenton until 4 A.M.

The soldiers began their march. Many did not have shoes. They marched barefoot through the snow. They left bloody footprints behind them. Washington saw that they would not get to Trenton in time to attack while it was still dark. Washington decided to keep going anyway.

Inside Trenton were 1,200 Hessian soldiers commanded by Colonel Johann Rall. Loyalists had warned Rall that the Americans might attack. But Rall did not believe that a large attack would come. He spent the night drinking heavily.

Washington's men met Hessian guards outside of Trenton at about 8 A.M. The Hessians fired and fell back. The Hessians in Trenton had enough warning to

A heroic painting of Washington crossing the Delaware. Many details are incorrect, but the giant 12-foot by 21-foot painting, first unveiled in 1850, remains the most famous picture of this event. One of the soldiers rowing the boat, right, is black. He is believed to be Prince Whipple, the bodyguard of one of Washington's aides and a slave who was promised his freedom in exchange for his army service.

Another view showing Washington on the New Jersey shore while boats ferry his small army across the Delaware.

get out of bed and form for battle in the streets. At that point the American artillery opened fire. A group of guns commanded by Alexander Hamilton fired down the street at the Hessians. From a different direction some Virginia infantry led by a very skilled officer named Hugh Mercer opened fire against the Hessian flank.

Four Hessian cannons fired back. Captain William Washington, a relative of George Washington, and Lieutenant James Monroe, a future president of the United States, led a charge against the Hessian guns. Both William Washington and Monroe were wounded, but their men captured the Hessian artillery. Colonel Rall bravely tried to rally his Hessians. He fell with a wound from which he later died (mortal wound).

Because it was storming, most of the infantry could not fire their muskets. That left the rebel artillery as the key

weapon. The rebels chased the Hessians through Trenton and trapped most of them in an orchard just outside of town. The surviving Hessians surrendered in the orchard.

The firing stopped. A messenger rode to Washington to tell him that the Hessians had surrendered. Washington shook his hand and said, "This is a most glorious day for our country."

The rebels lost very few casualties. The Hessians lost 106 killed or wounded and 918 prisoners. Washington had hoped to move on to Princeton and Brunswick. Since the other two rebel groups had not been able to cross the Delaware River, he ordered a retreat. Some of his soldiers did not make it back to camp until noon on December 27. Some had marched 40 miles, fought a battle, and not slept for 50 hours.

A famous historian, George Trevelyan, wrote about those men: never had so few men, in so short a time, had "greater or more lasting results upon the history of the world."

Top: Rebel artillery dominated the fighting at Trenton.

Above: James Monroe was a junior officer at Trenton. Monroe became the nation's fifth president.

The Battle of Princeton

After the Battle of Trenton about half of Washington's army went home. The remaining soldiers rested for two days before Washington led them back to Trenton. This time there was no fight in the town because the British had abandoned Trenton. Washington knew that most of his soldiers planned to leave the army the next day because their terms of enlistment were ending.

He tried to convince them to stay.

Washington rode to the front of a New England regiment. He described why the recent battle at Trenton was important. He told the men that if they would stay in the army for six more weeks, they would be giving the country a great service. He offered each soldier a $10 reward if they stayed. The regimental officers asked all volunteers to step forward at the sound of the drum. The drummer beat his drum. Not a man stepped forward!

Washington spoke again. He almost begged the soldiers to stay. The drummer beat his drum again. A few men stepped forward. More followed. Enough soldiers volunteered to give Washington a small army of about 1,600 men for six more weeks. Washington began planning a new advance, or offensive. He ordered all available rebel soldiers to gather at Trenton.

Meanwhile, Cornwallis collected his own force and marched quickly toward Trenton. He hoped to trap Washington and his army. On January 2, 1777, the British met the rebels outside of Trenton. The rebels' job was to slow the British advance. Most of the Americans fought well. Colonel Edward Hand led his Pennsylvania regiment with great skill. Hand's men forced the British to use up two valuable hours. Haussegger's German Battalion did poorly. The unit broke and ran, and Haussegger himself surrendered.

Night came. Cornwallis thought he had Washington trapped. He planned to attack and destroy the rebels the next day. In fact, Washington was in a bad spot. He did not have enough boats to retreat back over the Delaware River. There was no other place to retreat. Instead, Washington planned a bold move.

He ordered his men's campfires left burning to fool the British into thinking that the rebels were still in camp.

Gunners wrapped the wheels of the guns with rags so they would not make too much noise. Officers whispered orders to that the British could not hear. Everything was done so that the army could move secretly. Then, Washington led his men around the British flank.

While Cornwallis and his army slept, the rebels marched toward the British base at Princeton. A rebel spy had given Colonel Cadwalader a report of British positions in Princeton. Washington used that information to make a simple plan. He ordered Colonel Hugh Mercer to take 350 men to destroy a bridge. That would stop the British from escaping. Washington led the rest of his force by a side road toward the town.

George Washington at the Battle of Princeton.

Mercer's men were marching toward the bridge when they saw some British in a nearby orchard. Mercer turned his men to attack the British. Men had to stay calm and officers had to give clear orders so that a unit could change formation when the enemy was near. The fact that Mercer's men were able to do that showed how some Americans were becoming more like professional soldiers.

In the foreground a rebel cannon fires at a British battle line that has taken shelter behind a rail fence during the Battle of Princeton. In this painting Washington is riding toward the gun on a brown horse. American infantry duel with the British in the middle of the painting.

A sharp fight took place. The British infantry charged and drove back Mercer's men. Mercer himself fell with a mortal wound. For a moment it seemed as if the entire rebel force would rout, or run away. An American soldier wrote:

"At this moment Washington appeared in front of the American Army, riding towards those of us who were retreating, and exclaimed, 'Parade with us, my brave fellows! There is but a handful of the enemy and we will have them directly.'"

Washington led his soldiers toward the British. When the two sides were only 30 yards apart, Washington ordered his men to halt. Both sides fired. One of Washington's aides was "sure the General would fall and I raised my cloak over my face to shut out the dreadful sight."

The smoke cleared. Washington was still there, alive on his horse. The British broke and ran. The rebels marched into Princeton. There the British tried to defend the college buildings (College of New Jersey, the future Princeton University). Captain Alexander Hamilton brought up a cannon. After one shot the British surrendered.

The Battle of Princeton lasted about 45 minutes. The Americans lost 40 killed and wounded. The British lost 28 killed, 58 wounded, and about 190 missing and captured.

Back in Trenton, Cornwallis had heard the sounds of the fighting. He rushed his force toward Princeton. The rebels were just leaving the town when Cornwallis arrived.

Washington had hoped to continue his march to another British base at Brunswick. He knew that in Brunswick was the British war chest holding a lot of money. If he could capture the war chest, it would be a great blow against the British. But Washington also knew that his men were very tired since they had been up and moving or fighting all through the night and on into the day. So, Washington marched his men off to safety where they could rest.

The next day the Americans marched toward Morristown, New Jersey. They reached Morristown on January 5 and 6 and went into winter quarters.

Because Morristown was on the British flank, General Howe abandoned all of central and western New Jersey. The British were left with only two posts: Brunswick and Amboy. At Trenton and Princeton the British army had lost 1,250 men. The battles also stopped any idea of an easy advance to capture Philadelphia the next year.

During the New York campaign Washington had made many mistakes. Then Washington acted boldly and with great skill in the nine-day-long Trenton-Princeton

George Washington at Princeton.

Campaign. Frederick the Great of Prussia, one of history's greatest soldiers, heard about the campaign. He described Washington's campaign as one of the most brilliant in military history.

After many defeats the rebel army had won two battles. Success gave the soldiers and Washington himself confidence. The battles also changed attitudes throughout the colonies. A traveler reported, "The minds of the people are much [changed]. Their late successes have turned the scale and now they are all liberty mad again."

The battles discouraged General Howe. He saw that the Battle of Trenton had given the rebels "fresh courage." Howe wrote to London, "I do not now see a [chance] of [ending] the war, but by a [large battle] and I am aware of the difficulties in our way to [get a large battle]." Howe knew that in 1777 he would try to force the Americans to fight a large battle. But Howe also knew that Washington was very good at leading his army away from a fight.

The bad news about Trenton reached London in mid-February. King George gave his views to Lord North: "The surprise and want of spirit of the Hessian officers as well as soldiers at Trenton is not much to their credit." The king noted that before the battle the rebels had been demoralized. He expected that now the rebels were elated. But, if his generals used their British soldiers wisely, the king expected that they would defeat the rebels once and for all.

The news reached Paris, France. It delighted French leaders. France had suffered many defeats by the British. They liked it when British rebels defeated British soldiers.

Gains and Losses for 1776

As the year 1776 ended, both sides counted their gains and their losses. The British had captured New York City. From there they could sail up the Hudson River at any time. That made it difficult for the New England colonies to communicate with the rest of the colonies. On the other hand, the British discovered that they had to have a large force, or garrison, to defend New York.

To make the harbor safe, the British needed to hold Harlem Heights on Manhattan Island, Staten Island, Long Island, and Paulus Hook on the Jersey shore. Many soldiers had to defend those places. Every soldier on defense was one less who could attack the rebels.

The British also held Newport, Rhode Island. That

Washington leading his soldiers at the Battle of Princeton.

gave them a safe harbor for the fleet during winter storms. But Newport also required a big garrison to defend it, more men who could not attack the rebels.

A large British failure was the poor naval blockade of the American coast. In 1776 the British had 59 big warships for the campaign against the rebels. Fifteen had to guard the convoys that moved back and forth across the Atlantic. Another group helped the campaign in Canada. A large force of 23 warships worked with Howe's army in New York. Those many duties left only nine ships to blockade all of the ports from Connecticut to Maine.

So, the Royal Navy controlled the water wherever there was a British ship. But there were many places where there were no British ships. At those places American ships sailed to bring valuable cargoes to the American armies. Those American ships, called blockade runners because they sailed past the ships that blockaded the coast, were important. They departed French ports or neutral ports in the West Indies. They carried things that America did not make: muskets, cannons, and most importantly, gunpowder. Until the end of 1777 nine-tenths of all the rebel gunpowder came by blockade runner. Without that powder the rebellion would have failed.

During 1776 American fighting men had shown that they could become good soldiers. None were as good as the British regulars because they did not yet have enough discipline and training. So far, American generals had also shown that they needed to improve. Washington had grown as a leader. Benedict Arnold had shown that he might become a very good general. But most of the rest of the American generals still made too many mistakes. Between the senior, or high-ranking, generals and the fighting men were many junior, or lower-ranking, officers. Many of them showed real skill and bravery during 1776. The future seemed bright for officers like Henry Knox, Alexander Hamilton, Edward Hand, John Glover, William Washington, and John Cadwalader.

The campaign of 1776 had ended with the rebel victories of Trenton and Princeton. Those battles taught people in the colonies, in London, and in Paris something that surprised many people. They learned that if the American rebels kept trying, they had a fighting chance to gain their freedom.

Chronology

December 31, 1775: The Americans are badly beaten at the siege of Quebec. This is the beginning of the end for the invasion of Canada.

March 17, 1776: British troops evacuate Boston, leaving it to the Americans.

June 9-19, 1776: American troops give up on the invasion and flee Canada.

August 29, 1776: George Washington and his troops make a dangerous night-time retreat from Long Island, New York.

September 11, 1776: Three American congressmen meet with British officers for a so-called peace conference on Staten Island, New York.

September 16, 1776: After two recent defeats in the area the Americans fight well at the Battle of Harlem Heights in New York.

October 11, 1776: Benedict Arnold loses to the British navy in the Battle of Valcour Island, but delays the British from attacking further into New York.

November 16, 1776: The Americans suffer a bad defeat at the battle at Fort Washington, New York, and the Continental army flees New York. The Continental army starts to fall apart.

December 26, 1776: George Washington and his army win the Battle of Trenton, New Jersey.

January 3, 1777: Washington and his army surprise and defeat the British at the Battle of Princeton, New Jersey.

Glossary

AIDE: a soldier who works as an assistant to an officer

ARTILLERY: a group of cannons and other large guns used to help an army by firing at enemy troops

BATTALION: a battle-ready army unit made up of about 500 men

BLOCKADE: an effort to patrol the ocean to keep trading ships from entering or leaving a port

BOUNTY: a cash reward offered to men who join the military

CAMPAIGN: a series of military actions that are connected because they have the same goal

CASUALTIES: people killed, wounded, captured, or missing after a battle

ENLISTMENT: signing up to join an army or navy; a term of enlistment is the agreed time that one will stay in the military.

FEINT: a movement of troops meant to fool the enemy about what an army is doing

FLANK: one side of an army on a battlefield

GARRISON: the group of soldiers stationed at a fort or military post

GUERRILLAS: a small group of soldiers that makes sneak attacks in areas away from the large armies and battlefields

HESSIANS: hired German soldiers who fought for the British; so called because most of them were from a part of Germany called Hesse-Cassel

MERCENARIES: soldiers who get paid to fight for a foreign country

MORALE: fighting spirit, or willingness to fight. To become demoralized is to lose one's fighting spirit.

MORTAL WOUND: a wound that eventually leads to death

OUTFLANK: to move around the side, or flank, of the enemy troops on a battlefield

RAISE (AN ARMY): to build up a military force by getting new soldiers to enlist or by gathering soldiers from other units

RALLY: to encourage and reorganize soldiers who are about to lose their nerve and rout (run away) from a battlefield

REAR GUARD: troops guarding the rear of a marching or fighting army. A fight by the rear guard is called a rearguard action.

REGULATIONS: the printed official rules for all aspects of soldier behavior, army life, and conduct of military actions

REINFORCEMENTS: additional soldiers sent to help an army either before or during a battle

SKIRMISH: a brief battle involving a small number of soldiers

STRATEGY: the overall plan for a battle or campaign

SUPPLY LINE: the route used to bring supplies from the base to an army in the field

TROOP SHIPS: navy ships that carry troops on the ocean to where they are needed

Further Resources

Books:

Adams, Russell B., Jr., ed. *The Revolutionaries*. Alexandria, VA: Time-Life Books, 1996.

Bliven, Bruce, Jr. *The American Revolution*. New York: Random House, 1986.

Boatner, Mark M., III. Encyclopedia of the American Revolution. Mechanicsburg, PA: Stackpole Books, 1994.

Brenner, Barbara. *If You Were There in 1776*. New York: Bradbury Press, 1994. Details of daily life in the rebellious colonies in 1776.

Dolan, Edward F. *The American Revolution: How We Fought the War of Independence*. Brookfield, CT: Millbrook Press, 1995.

Fleming, Thomas. *First in Their Hearts: A Biography of George Washington*. Lakeville, CT: Grey Castle Press, 1984.

Kaye, Harvey J. *Thomas Paine: Firebrand of the Revolution*. New York: Oxford University Press, 2000.

Martin, J. P. *Private Yankee Doodle*. Fort Washington, PA: Eastern Acorn Press, 1998. The entire diary of Joseph Plumb Martin, who enlisted in the Continental army when he was 15.

Murphy, Jim. *A Young Patriot: The American Revolution as Experienced by One Boy*. New York: Clarion Books, 1996. Based on the life story of a real person, Joseph Plumb Martin, who was 15 years old when he enlisted in the Continental Army.

Peacock, Louise. *Crossing The Delaware: A History in Many Voices*. New York: Atheneum, 1998.

Websites:

http://library.thinkquest.org/10966/
The Revolutionary War—A Journey Towards Freedom

ushistory.org/march/index.html
Virtual Marching Tour of the American Revolution

http://www.pbs.org/ktca/liberty/game/index.html
The Road to Revolution—A Revolutionary Game

http://www.pbs.org/ktca/liberty/chronicle/index.html
Chronicle of the Revolution
Read virtual newspapers of the Revolutionary era

Places to Visit:

Morristown National Historical Park, Morristown, New Jersey
Winter quarters for the Continental army 1776–1777

Museum of American History, Smithsonian Institution,
Washington, DC
One of Benedict Arnold's ships that was sunk at the Battle of
Valcour Island is on exhibit, with a cannonball still lodged in its
side.

Washington Crossing State Park, Washington Crossing (near
Trenton), New Jersey
The spot where George Washington and his army crossed the
Delaware River in 1776

About the Authors

James R. Arnold has written more than 20 books on military
history topics and contributed to many others. Roberta Wiener
has coauthored several books with Mr. Arnold and edited
numerous educational books, including a children's encyclopedia.
They live and farm in Virginia.

Set Index

Bold numbers refer to volumes; *italics* refer to illustrations

Acknowledgments

Eldridge S. Brooks, *The Century Book of the American Revolution*, 1897: 49B

Anne S. K. Brown Military Collection, John Hay Library, Brown University, Providence, Rhode Island: Title page, 11, 35, 36L, 48, 56

Architect of the Capitol: 62,

John Batchelor: 38

Charles C. *Coffin Boys of '76*, 1876: 28

Harper's New Monthly Magazine: 16

J. G. Heck. *Iconographic Encyclopedia of Science, Literature, and Art*, 1851: 8–9

The Historical Society of Pennsylvania, 60–61, *Battle of Princeton*, by William Mercer

Independence National Historical Park: 52, 57B

Library of Congress:, 8, 12–13, 17, 18B, 25, 26–27, 30, 32, 33, 36–37, 40, 41, 45, 50

Maryland National Guard: 46

Military Archive & Research Services, England: 24

National Archives: 10, 20T, 22, 34, 42, 49T, 51, 53, 55, 57T, 58–59

National Archives of Canada: 18T, 19T

National Park Service: 6–7 artist Lloyd K. Townsend

U.S. Marine Corps, Washington D.C.: 20B *Defeat on Lake Champlain 13 October 1776*, by Charles Waterhouse, 64–65 *Marines with Washington at Princeton 3 January 1777*, by Charles Waterhouse

U.S. Naval Academy Museum, 30–31 *Forcing the Hudson River Passage*, by Domonic Serres

U.S. Naval Historical Center, Washington, D.C.: 19B, 21, 38–39

U.S. Government Printing Office: Front cover

Maps by Jerry Malone